THEY SPEAK

For ah! we know not what each other says,
These things and I; in sound *I* speak—
Their sound is but their stir, they speak by silences.

Francis Thompson: *The Hound of Heaven*

THEY SPEAK BY SILENCES

By a Carthusian

Translated from the French
by a Monk of Parkminster

DARTON · LONGMAN + TODD

First published in 1955 by Longmans, Green and Co Ltd

This edition published in 1996 by
Darton, Longman and Todd Ltd
1 Spencer Court
140–142 Wandsworth High Street
London SW18 4JJ

ISBN 0–232–52173–5

Imprimi potest: Fr Ferdinandus
Prior Cartusiae
In domo Cartusiae: viii Decembris MCMLIV

Nihil obstat: Dermitius Fogarty, S.T.D.
Censor deputatus
Imprimatur: H. Gibney
Vicarius Generalis
Southwarci: die xxiv Junii MCMLV

A catalogue record for this book is available
from the British Library

Phototypeset by Intype London Ltd, London
Printed and bound in Great Britain
Redwood Books, Trowbridge, Wiltshire

CONTENTS

◡◠

vii

FOREWORD

∽∾

THE FOLLOWING PAGES ARE A TRANSLATION OF TWO small books published originally in French by the Benedictine nuns of St Priscilla in Rome. The first, *Silence Cartusien*, was published in 1948, there being nothing to indicate its origin beyond a brief foreword in Italian which ran as follows:

> The thoughts contained in this little book were from the pen of one who, in the silence of the Charterhouse, had already arrived at the summits of the spiritual heights, and dwelt there unceasingly. Souls who have reached such perfection in this life are rare; not so rare, however, are those who ardently aspire thereto. It is chiefly for such as these—to encourage and help them to arrive at those same heights—that these thoughts have been preserved and collected.

Hidden in its origin and intention, the book nevertheless soon began to make its influence felt in Italy and in France, and the first edition was soon exhausted. A second edition appeared and then a third, and it is the welcome it received abroad that has suggested that it may be equally welcomed in this country. A very appreciative review of it appeared in *La Vie Spirituelle* in 1950,* in which the writer said: '. . . This little book which

*Hélène Lubienska de Lenval, *Du Silence*, October 1950.

ix

I have just brought back with me from Rome will not be found in any library nor in any catalogue. It was only by chance that I discovered it in the catacombs of St Priscilla in Rome, when I questioned the nuns as to their work. Mentioning their printing press, they showed me amongst other books this little volume. No name, either of author or editor . . . When questioned, the good nuns replied simply: "*E un certosino morte da poco* . . . the author was a Carthusian who died not long ago".' That was all they knew.

The book in question was followed in 1953—always with the same anonymity—by a similar work by the same hand, *Voix Cartusienne*; and it is these two works which are now translated and presented in English for the first time.

They were born in silence and solitude of a Charterhouse, and their very anonymity is part of that silence.

It is due perhaps to the reader to say—and it is all we can say—that the writer of these pages held for some years various positions of authority in the Carthusian Order, involving the direction of souls. The extracts here given were never in the author's mind intended for publication; only after his death in 1945 were they carefully collected and published as has already been told. The titles of the chapters are not titles in the strict sense of the word, but are simply words taken from the text of each chapter, and even the chapters themselves have been arbitrarily divided as we give them. In the original they followed no special order, and were written at different times.

Such in brief is all that is known to the outside world of the writer of this book. His life, like the life of any Carthusian, was not made up of external events, and we need do no more than let his words speak for themselves. As he himself would be the first to admit, it is not what they say but what they leave unsaid that will probably influence other souls, seeking as he sought that union with God which is not peculiar to Carthusians or to any other religious, but is the end set before all men. We can only re-echo the hope expressed by the original editor of these works that the thoughts preserved and collected in this little book may help and encourage others to persevere in the ascent to that union.

Our thanks are due to a Carmelite nun, who for obvious reasons would wish to remain unknown, who provided the first draft of the translation.

St Hugh's Charterhouse,
Parkminster, Sussex.
Feast of St. Andrew, 1954.

Carthusian Silence

∽∽

OUR SILENCE IS NOT JUST EMPTINESS AND death. On the contrary, it should draw ever nearer, and bring us nearer, to the fullness of life. We are silent because the words by which our souls would fain live cannot be expressed in earthly language.

We Speak to God

∽∾∽

... YOU KNOW THAT WHAT OUR CARTHUSIAN lips do not utter and what our pens have not the time to write, we say to God for those whom we love. Our silence is not a silence of death: rather it is the sacred stillness of a sanctuary. Our little houses, like our souls, are occupied by Someone. *Magister adest et vocat te . . . The Master is here, and calleth thee.* He is the Master: He has a right to everything. He takes our hours, one by one, and fills them. But He allows—nay more, He commands—us to see in Him those who are also *in sinu suo*—in His bosom. To think of them is a duty to which we would be bound, even if it did not appeal to us.

I find much consolation in making my spiritual reading in . . . There I experience the joy of coming into actual contact with those great works through words which in no way detract from them. This is so important! Words are not merely the outer shell, they are the body itself, and between that body and that soul there is a substantial union. The soul is necessary for that body, and that body is necessary for the soul. If one is wanting, the substantial whole is wanting. All that remains is but one element of its being, and the whole as such fails to materialize. And this applies to all our ideas: they really only live when they are expressed, and you know that it is in acts that their adequate expression lies. Only then do they find their fulfilment.

Silence is Not Forgetfulness

༺༻

SILENCE IS NOT FORGETFULNESS. IN THE Charterhouse we believe this, and our whole endeavour is to live it. And so the thought of you has filled these long months of silence, and has found expression in that inner speech which does not break silence but gives it its value and life. I do not need to tell you that this living and life-giving speech comes to you daily from many hearts in this house of peace and joy so familiar to you. Distances no longer count, and contacts by invisible waves which speed across the world in an instant are now part of everyday life. And when these waves are sent out by friendship and, spreading in every direction, are received by friendship too, what limits are there to what they can do?

The great truth that the Holy Spirit utters in the depths of our soul 'in unspeakable groanings' is that the Infinite God is present there, living and loving, and offering Himself to us unceasingly, as Truth to the mind and Charity to the heart; and that we have only to make an act of faith in order to possess Him and enter into relations of eternal love with Him. *Qui credit in me habet vitam aeternam . . . hath* eternal life. The present tense fits exactly.

There Lies our Whole Vocation

‿◯‿

. . . Poor brother, who thinks he is forgotten and is not forgotten at all, but who himself
forgets that the memory that lies in the heart
cannot always express itself outwardly, and that
the number of unexpressed things far exceeds
those that are expressed. The Carthusian life rests
upon a deep foundation of silence which you know
and love, and it is in that depth that the Eternal
Word is born for each one of us. There lies our
whole vocation: to listen to Him Who generates
the Word and to live thereby. The Word proceeds
from Silence, and we strive to find Him in His
Source. This is because the Silence here in question is not a void nor a negation but, on the contrary, Being at Its fullest and most fruitful
plenitude. That is why It generates; and that is
why we keep silent. I read somewhere that books
are of more value for what they do not say than
for what they do. The reader is like a man gazing
at an horizon. Beyond the outlines that he sees,
he seeks perspectives he barely discerns, but which
draw him precisely because of the mystery he
senses in them. So the books one loves are those
which make one think. One seeks in them that
silence whence the words were born, which is
those depths of the soul which no language can

5

express, for they are beyond expression. It is here we touch what is measureless, eternal and divine in us.

Distant Scenes

❧

WHAT ENCHANTS ME IN THESE PAGES AND CON-
stitutes their perfection is that they are not content
with merely charming our finer senses by the sheer
beauty of the words, or by the harmony of their
phrasing; nor yet with satisfying the mind by the
soundness or even the loftiness of the ideas they
convey. They awaken those deeper regions of the
soul where God dwells, by which the soul can be
united to Him. But they contact them in the only
way in which they can do: by touches, that is,
barely perceptible and, as it were, spiritualized,
which resemble as far as is possible His approaches
Who is there, wholly present beyond the pale of
our words.

These are what one may call 'distant scenes':
the overtones of a picture; and we need them.
We intuitively know that reality is greater than
ourselves, and that no words of ours can ever
adequately express that reality. We can make
others sense it, but we can never convey it to them
in words. Anyone who thinks he can understand
it fully is lessening both it and us. Anyone, on the
other hand, who has caught some glimpse of its
mystery and helps us to share that vision, makes
us, along with himself, greater.

Carthusian Joy

∽∾∽

... ALL THESE MISERIES WHICH CRISS-CROSS
our lives are at bottom of little account... It is
only the surface of the soul which has been slightly
ruffled; the depths have remained untroubled. Alas
for us that we do not live sufficiently in those
depths where peace reigns, but far too much on
the surface where we get disturbed. There you
have the true secret of our Carthusian calm and
joy. The daily upsets of hurt and wounded feelings
are found no less among us than anywhere else.
They form part of our existence here below, and
we are still living in this world! But we do not let
them distress us. A whole part of ourselves
emerges from and dominates them, and all our
endeavour is to live by this loftier part. It is there
we preserve our serenity of soul; and it is there that
our 'palm tree in the desert' grows, beneath the
shade of which we rest 'in peace'.

Our Capacity for Joy

WHAT ATTRACTS US IN THE *IMITATION* AND
delights us in Thomas à Kempis (and, above all,
in St Augustine) is that Someone Who is greater
than they; greater than everyone and everything.
And that Someone wounds our soul with a wound
which will never heal, and it is through that
wound that He finds His way to the very centre of
our being. But obviously He can only take possession there by displacing us, and that means that
we shall suffer greatly. So much the better! Our
capacity for joy is measured by our capacity for
suffering, and it will be because we have suffered
greatly that one day we shall know great happiness.

Humility

∽∾

SUFFERING IS GOOD: GUARD IT AS A PRECIOUS thing. Far better than any words of ours can do, it makes known to God the soul's need for Him. What causes our suffering is the disproportion we see between what we are and what He is. A soul would be petty, indeed, if it did not suffer from that knowledge. But this suffering diminishes that disproportion, and comes from the very effort we are making to reach Him. With the effort, however, is given grace: *Humilibus dat gratiam . . . He giveth grace to the humble.* There you have true humility, and it is the reason for all the graces we have received (and they are much greater than we realize). Humility acknowledges these graces: it would not be true humility if it did not. *What hast thou that thou hast not received?* St Paul does not overlook the *hast*, and we must never forget it either. But he reminds us that all that we have received is the gift of God – we have *received* it. And what we have received is the pledge of what we shall receive. We must never mind facing our misery, but we should always bring it to God's mercy, which is ever inclined towards it in order to raise it up.

၁၇၁

... DESPITE THE PETTY MISERIES INSEPAR-
able from human nature, our houses remain
havens of prayer and of true recollection. We are
neither heroes nor saints as some lofty souls
believe, who credit us with the ideal richness of
their own interior life. But neither are we idle or
useless folk. We quicken our Offices and our spiritual exercises with a real spirit of love, and with a
desire to dedicate our whole life to that spirit.

∽∽

... ACTUALLY, THERE IS NOTHING REALLY new, for we strive to live—unhappily not sufficiently—in that eternity, 'ever ancient, ever new'. We lose in its depths our cares and troubles, for they are all only passing, whereas we are made for what is lasting and abiding.

God loves us more than we realize or can ever repay Him. Remember weakness is no hindrance to love: in our relations with God it is even an enormous strength. Let us remain, then, united in weakness, in prayer, and in the desire to belong wholly to God.

How God Acts

‿‿

YOU HAVE A RIGHT, NOT MERELY TO THE crumbs but to the table. But it is by our prayers, far more than by our words or letters, that we satisfy that right. Our whole life is a life of prayer and silence, and it is there that our value and activity lie. You know that, and you are not surprised, therefore, that our words are brief and our letters rare. We offer up instead our long Offices, and that life of continuous prayer which is our aim, and it is this you receive from all at San Francesco.

Sensible joy, when God gives it, is indeed sweet, but it is not essential, and it would be harmful when He withdraws it. Take, then, what He gives—that is all that matters. Love does not always heed the desires of those whom it loves. It knows what is good for them and procures it for them, and satisfies their desires provided they are in accordance with that good. That is how God acts. Do not forget that God is Love. We should live with this great truth constantly before us.

Space

∽∽

... For us, space is only an 'accident', and after time the most difficult to define and perceive, while unions are substantial: that is to say, constant and immutable. This is because there are within us vaster regions of the soul, where we no longer reason or argue, but see and taste and love.

Live, then, rather in these depths. They are the kingdom of peace, because they are the abode of the God of peace. There you have the unchanging meeting-place of our unions.

Ego Sum Vita

∽∽

... I AM NO LATINIST, BUT WITHOUT EVER having had the curiosity to justify what I am going to say, I have always associated the word 'manet' with 'mansio'. I have always translated the text: *Qui manet in caritate, in Deo manet et Deus in eo* by *He who hath his dwelling-place in Love hath his dwelling-place in God* (*Who is Love*), *and he is himself the dwelling-place of God*. We must be in that dwelling-place and of it ... we must see life in death. In a word, we have life because Jesus died, and in the measure in which we share in His death. And the reason is: *Ego sum Vita ... I am the Life*.

Darkness Becomes Light

❦

... It is not in the light of words that we must seek light. The light of a word is still something created, ephemeral—part of our nothingness. If we become attached to that light, we are halting on the way; we shall never reach the goal. That is why God bestows on souls whom He loves the grace of refusing them this light. He leaves them in darkness, and it is that darkness that becomes light: *And night shall be my light in my pleasures.*

The true light shines in the darkness, but one must get accustomed to finding it there. At first one is terrified: light is such a lovely and necessary thing. But, little by little, the day begins to dawn, and one sees that the light we miss is an inferior light, whilst that which is growing is much purer.

The light which is lacking at these times is our own light. We no longer perceive our state of grace, or rather we do not feel it. We no longer find within us that soothing assurance of belonging to God. What we do find in ourselves is division and darkness.

We must go beyond this stage. We must get out of ourselves, and despise the voice that doubts or argues or despairs. We must listen to that other voice which speaks to us from the depths of our

16

soul, and says to us: 'God is Love: to be separated from Him there must be an act of the faculty of loving—a love opposed to His love. I do not see that in myself; therefore . . .'

That is the true light, the light that shines in the darkness. But because it does shine in the darkness, we have to pass through these hours of darkness, hours when one says: 'My God, I do not see that I have willed to offend you, but I am no longer conscious of my love for you. I no longer feel the attachment of my will to your Goodness, or taste the union of my spirit with your Truth. But I do know that to offend you one must will to do so, and since I do not wish that, then I believe that I have not done so'.

We must be content with this single light from within, and attach ourselves to it alone—the light of Him Who is the Voice or Word. That is why all other voices must be stilled. Even when they make themselves heard, they do not speak to us; they no longer tell us anything. God closes the ear that is conscious of them, in order that He may open the ear which listens to the voice from within.

The divine Will—that is our true light, and it is the light of Love. The soul desiring this Will knows that it is in Truth and holiness, even if everything else cries out to it that it is in error and evil.

Light from on High

∽∾

... But this light is from on high. Here below, we catch only its furtive rays, like those which find their way through an autumn mist. And we suffer, because we are made for the 'light of life'—eternal light. But that is where we err; for the mist, the darkness and the anxiousness are all part of the divine plan which leads to the supreme light. We must believe before we see: we must believe in Him Who sees, if we would one day see what He sees and as He sees. God has willed it thus, and He finds joy and glory therein.

A soul who sees nothing but darkness but says to Him: 'My God, I see nothing; but because you tell me that this darkness is your light, I believe it. Everything in me tells me the contrary, but I give up this "me" and listen to you rather than to it. I choose you and not it': such a soul puts God in His true place—the first.

It is clear that this is the hardest sacrifice of all. *Abneget semetipsum . . . let him deny himself.* For reason which tells me that 'this is darkness' is the very citadel of self; and when one surrenders that, one surrenders everything. *And night shall be my light in my pleasures.* Once accepted, this darkness, which reason calls darkness (but which God calls light), at once begins to glow, and becomes the lovely radiance of the approaching dawn of eternity.

Believe, then, that in this topsy-turvy world in which we have to live, in this world so bereft of peace and so far from God —above all in our soul, that soul so crushed—GOD IS PRESENT: loving, giving Himself, pouring His peace into souls of good will . . .

Believe this, I say, not trying to understand it nor seeking to feel it. For to believe is precisely to give one's assent to a word without understanding or feeling. Believe: and that very Word, the Word of God, will transform us into Himself, and make us partakers in His Life.

By Faith We Perceive Divine Truth

~∞~

FROM TIME TO TIME, GOD ALLOWS PEACE TO
well up from the spiritual depths of the soul and
to pervade our sensitive nature, where it finds
expression in sensible sweetness. But it is only felt
at certain times because it is the habitual atmosphere of that secret part of ourselves that we call
the summit of our soul. There is, as it were, a
sudden up-spring which makes us conscious of it,
because it then invades the more superficial parts
of the soul, to which our gaze can penetrate more
readily. Its presence in the depths of the soul is
much more difficult to perceive, and to apprehend
it calls for a faculty adapted to the purpose. This
faculty we have, but we are not sufficiently accustomed to using it: it is faith. It is by faith that
we perceive divine Truth, and in particular the
presence and action of God within us; just as
the eye perceives colour and form, and the mind
the intelligible aspects of objects which we term
ideas. Faith introduces us into another and higher
world, that of God of which it is the light.

Ask Jesus, then, to make this wonderful light
shine more and more in our hearts—this light
which, little by little, becomes love, and which is
the true life, the *lumen vitae*.

With God, Infallibility is Not the Same as Necessity

∽∾

HERE IS YOUR DIFFICULTY: GOD GIVES EVERY-thing—the power to will, to act, and to persevere. Wherein, then, lies our merit or moral responsibility?

I reply: moral responsibility lies in the free acceptance by man of this complete gift. This acceptance by man, like everything else, is the gift of God. But that does not prevent it from being free: because God, in giving us these things, respects the free nature of the being on whom He bestows them. Man accepts, then, by the normal play of his nature, intelligent and voluntary (which is what liberty is), and he is responsible for his acceptance or refusal.

What worries us, perhaps, is that this free acceptance takes place infallibly. But infallibly does not mean necessarily. A necessary act is an act which is imposed on us, either by a force outside us, or by our nature. An infallible act is one which will take place inevitably, because it is part of a plan which evokes it but which nevertheless comes about freely, since human liberty is also part of that plan. Free acts foreseen by God come to pass infallibly, because they are part of a fore-knowledge which cannot err. On the other hand, they take place freely, because that fore-knowledge sees them and wills them as free acts. We do good or evil as God has foreseen that we shall; but what we do is free, because God has likewise foreseen it as free.

Our efforts to explain these things can go no further. Beyond that is an abyss wherein the light of reason fades, as the light of faith grows and increases, because it is discovering the majesty of Him in Whom it believes.

Mysteries

MYSTERIES ARE NOT DARK SHADOWS, BEFORE which we must shut our eyes and be silent. On the contrary, they are dazzling splendours, with which we ought to sate our gaze, whilst recognizing, however, that they extend far beyond its capacity, and that our eyes cannot bear their full radiance. It is in contemplating them, in speaking of them, that we dispose ourselves to be given even here below as much of them as God sees fit to impart to us, and to receive one day that fullness of light which will be the essence of our beatitude.

True Detachment

∽∾∽

TOO OFTEN PEOPLE IMAGINE THAT CHRISTIAN detachment consists in loving nothing. This is terribly wrong. Never has there been a heart more loving than the heart of Jesus, and our hearts should be modelled on His. To love is the great, indeed the only, commandment. *This is the first commandment . . . thou shalt love the Lord thy God with thy whole heart . . . and thy neighbour.* There you have the whole Gospel, the whole of life, the whole of God, Who is Love itself. Love, yes: but an ordered love, which is a living and communicating force, capable of immolating everything that prevents it from giving itself.

And this immolation to Love of all that is not love is what we call detachment. Detachment, then, is the negative side of attachment (or love). It is detachment which 'sets in order' our loves. *Ordinavit in me caritatem* . . . He has *set in order* charity in me. The God of Love, living in a soul, causes it to love all other beings, in so far as they participate in Him, Who is Being. The soul must love them as God loves them—that is to say, in the same way as God gives Himself to them. It is this gift of Infinite Being to a finite being that gives it life, and is the measure of our love. Our love, measured by God Himself and by what we find of

Him in His works, is an ordered love. This being so, there must be no attachments which are not in conformity with this rule. If the soul finds any such within itself, it does not suppress them, it disciplines them. This idea of order is at the root of everything. Detachment is the condition of order, just as order is the condition of love. And that is why it can be said that detachment is 'ordered love'.

Corporal Asceticism

༄

DISCIPLINE (OR MORTIFICATION) PUTS BACK in its place that something in us which should serve but wants to rule. That is to say, it restores that order which has been upset by the Fall. It puts reason back again as the rule of life; it makes us calm and reasonable. If it does not tend to do this, then it is stupid and pointless.

Mortification of the body is above all a symbol. It stands for that chastisement which the will should have the courage to inflict on all the powers of the soul, in order to submit them, along with itself, to God, and so re-establish in Him that shattered unity of our human nature. That is the goal, most sublime and blessed, of all our efforts: a goal which is well worth the journeying, however hard it may be.

God's Moments

∽∿∽

... OUR THANKSGIVING TO GOD BECOMES A note in the immense spiritual harmony which hymns His goodness.

The realization of our soul's grievous need is another note of the same hymn, and not one of the least beautiful. Here we are in a minor key. There is a kind of veil over the soul, and this veil diffuses sadness over all her praise. One needs courage, and above all confidence, to go on singing. Do your best to possess this courage, this confidence. Our times of powerlessness are God's moments. He has all the glory, for it is He Who does everything, and what He does fills us with wonder.

We suffer at such times, because we would like to share in His glory by sharing in the work He is doing. We do not realize that God wants all because He is all; and that He keeps us in a state of nothingness because that is all we are. And so we enter upon Truth and Life.

That is why the saints gloried in these hours of anguish. *When I am weak, then am I powerful ... Gladly will I glory in my infirmities, that the power of Christ may dwell in me.* Note the *that*: it is conjunctive; it links two things—'my infirmities' and 'the power of Christ'.

Don't be surprised, then, if you feel weak and wretched, and don't let it worry you. It is the very condition of strength—true, divine, strength—but it is not a thing that is felt. Now possession, without the feeling of possessing, does not satisfy us. We are made not only for the Good and True, but for the enjoyment of the Good and True. And we shall enjoy them. The day will come without fail, provided we know how to accept in this life possession without joy, in reparation for our former excessive delight in, and our too eager desire for, pleasure.

We Must View Things from Above

ꙮ

WE MUST VIEW MEN AND THINGS FROM ABOVE, just as God Himself sees them, Who in His infinite plan makes the greater things stand out in contrast to the lesser. This wide and comprehensive view is good for us, and puts us in our true perspective. We form part of an immense choir, and our part is a very beautiful one, and we must fulfil it to the best of our ability. There are, however, other parts in God's plan which also have their beauty, and which, although they are dissonant, resolve themselves in harmony. You have noticed the wonderful sense of peace in the final perfect resolution following a seventh or ninth chord. Good Friday was a broken chord, which was a preparation for the final resolution. Such times are composed chiefly of ninth chords, and we must know how to accept them in order to enjoy our eternal rest.

The Life of the Soul

∽∾

WE MUST NOT BE SURPRISED IF WE DO NOT SEE the progress that our soul makes. One never sees life, least of all the higher life of the spirit: one believes it. We believe that God wants to give Himself to us, because He is Love—that is, essentially the gift of self. And when He finds a soul that wants to belong to Him, He gives Himself. The life of the soul, fundamentally, is this faith. Then gradually it communicates itself to our exterior life, and expresses itself in act, little by little, slowly, secretly . . . in the same way that our ideas are realized.

Nothing Unites so Much as Sacrifice

∽∾

Do not seek too eagerly to feel God's assistance. Feeling is like the fragrance of our eternal homeland, perceived through the veil of faith. To reward or encourage us, God allows from time to time a foretaste of this happiness to reach us, but it is only incidental and momentary. By all means accept it and enjoy it when He sends it, but make a willing sacrifice of it when He withholds it. When we make the sacrifice, it is we who give Him *una fragranza*—the perfume so dear to His Heart. We shall find it again in that land where nothing is lost. It is then we shall appreciate the one saying of Jesus which St Paul has preserved for us: *It is more blessed to give than to receive*. The essence of our relations with God here below is faith: faith in His Love, which is His Being and His Life. *And we have believed . . . in His love*. Nothing unites so much as sacrifice. It offers up as a holocaust all narrowness in us. At the same time, it makes us greater, and so makes room for God Who is so great, and Who loves us with all the immensity of His infinite love.

Sensitiveness

⌣⌣

SENSITIVENESS AND EXTREME DELICACY OF feeling are a treasure. They constitute the richness of a nature: but they also constitute its torment!

Moreover, they are a danger. For sensitiveness is not controlled by itself: it must look for and find its guide in reason. If it does this, it completes reason in a most wonderful way, by giving it vitality and warmth, without which reason remains cold and sterile. But if sensitiveness is not controlled by reason, it becomes the source of every kind of wandering and caprice.

How can we subject it to the guidance of reason? There are two ways, which are not actually exclusive or independent of one another, but are ordered and complementary. The one is in the natural order, the other in the supernatural. The former belongs to psychology, and is called the training of the will, self-mastery, the discipline of the passions. For those who have not undertaken this training at the outset of life (and unfortunately that is the greater number nowadays), it consists in gradual, regular exercises, thoroughly and perseveringly followed, by which one acquires the habit of submitting every movement of our sensitive nature to the control of reason. How well we know this task! We have attempted it, but perhaps it has not yielded all the results we anticipated. For subjective reasons, which may be countless and are always difficult to disentangle, it often happens that our sensitive nature rebels, and the effort to subdue it only serves to stimulate it.

This is where supernatural means come in, and offer a solution at once profound and simple, and most effective in restoring our peace of soul. The supernatural motives are those of GOD WITHIN US. God has in view only His own glory, which is to give Himself to us, and to show Himself both great and good in so doing. Our souls should have no other end than this—to make known this same greatness and goodness, or better, this great goodness, for the greatness of God consists in being infinitely good. That is what God wants in the depths of the soul, and that is what the soul ought to want, too, in order to unite itself to Him, and thus find its serenity and strength.

Now there are some souls who are destined to glorify God by a sensitiveness more delicate and vibrant, the subjection of which to reason demands much greater efforts, and remains moreover always more or less imperfect. St Augustine was one of these souls. For such souls mere disciplinary effort is not enough, and in many cases remains ineffective. To this effort they must add the calm and grateful acceptance of the temperament God has given them: it is by this acceptance they will glorify God. They must see in their powerlessness to suppress—often even to control—their sensitiveness, a means of submission to the designs of divine Providence, conceived as they are by a God Who is Love, and carried out by the all-mighty Father.

This is because union with God, which is the source of divine peace in the soul, does not necessarily imply natural human perfection. Such union consists in perfect conformity with God's designs upon us. A soul can be supernaturally perfect— and consequently at peace—and yet have many natural imperfections. This is particularly the case with a temperament which is persistently over-impressionable, and which vibrates to every breath from without, while the heart feels and echoes these vibrations. It is sufficient for the soul to accept this state of things and to make a constant effort, simple, calm and confident, day by day, to keep under control this lower part, and to submit it to the guidance of reason, and above all to that of faith.

For that is what constitutes forgetfulness of self and abandonment to God. To forget oneself does not mean not thinking of oneself, but thinking of oneself to the extent willed by God. God wills that, for the life of both soul and body, we should take certain measures indicated by reason and approved on a higher plane by faith with a view to a supernatural end. Not to do so is neither to abandon oneself to God nor to forget oneself, but to tempt God and to depart from His designs. We abandon ourselves when, having taken these measures, we pay no heed to the results, but leave it to God to bring them about or not, as He pleases. This is true abandonment, which glorifies God, and brings peace to the soul. *Glory to God in the highest, and on earth peace to men of good will.* The real good will is that of Him Who is Goodness itself and Love itself. A human will is good in so far as it identifies itself in all things with that Will.

Daily Crosses

~∞~

TRY NOT TO BE UNDULY DISTURBED BY THE tiny incidents of life. There is nothing permanent in them. Our soul is immeasurably greater than all these things. Part of its greatness is precisely its power to pass beyond all these ephemeral disturbances and to reach out and touch the eternal through what is merely passing. The causes—or occasions rather—of our troubles are only instruments; what we must try to do is to see the One Who is handling them—the God of Love.

It is the spirit of faith that sees this Love in suffering, and turns its darkness into light. This light of love—in reality the light of the Holy Spirit—is what imparts sweetness and goodness to everything. Our daily crosses are the disciplinary exercises by which the Holy Spirit develops in a soul the habit of using this light.

Suffering

✌

SUFFERING COMES WITHIN THE SCOPE OF
God's Will for us. By accepting it lovingly, the soul
unites itself to that Will, and becomes one with
Him Whose Will is His Being.

Why does God so often call us along this road,
where we meet Him more surely than anywhere
else? Because it is a mark of His special love for
us. These are our 'trysting-places' with Him.
Thank Him for them, then, and be faithful in
keeping them. To be faithful does not mean that
we shall not suffer. One of our greatest illusions is
to imagine that we suffer badly because we suffer.

Suffering is, and always will be, suffering—that
is, violence done to our nature. Even God cannot
change that. *Thou hast made us for Thyself* . . . It is
in the 'Thyself' that lies our happiness. Suffering
is in opposition to the 'Thou hast made' and to
the movement towards our end, 'Thyself'.

By suffering with us and for us, Jesus has
brought this opposition into the movement
towards Himself. Suffering has become the way,
but only (to use a philosophical term) *per accidens*.
In its essence, and taken by itself, suffering
remains in opposition, hostile. It is only when we
have waged war against it and mastered it, and

have proved ourselves superior to it by bearing it, that it becomes an instrument and a servant.

Go on, then, bearing suffering bravely, making it serve to enlarge your capacity for the divine life in you. Continue, too, to look upon God with love when He sends you these hours which mean so much for our spiritual growth—when our crushed heart can do little more than utter its *Fiat*.

Our Suffering Should Always Remain Calm

∽∾

... Try to rise above suffering. It is a state of soul which springs from the best that is in us.

It comes from a desire to belong more and more wholly to God, and to fuse our very life with His. This desire is excellent, and we should grieve when we see it being realized so slowly and imperfectly. Our suffering, however, should always remain calm, and ever turned towards the tranquillizing rays of a joy superior to it. The suffering is due to our fallen state, whereas the joy comes from the goodness of God. Now God is good infinitely more than we are bad. The joy is the term and end for which we were made; suffering is merely one aspect of the way. *My peace I give unto you ... These things I have spoken to you, that my joy may be in you, and your joy may be filled*. You know what the words *These things I have spoken to you* mean. Jesus had just said: *As the Father hath loved me, I also have loved you. Abide in my love*. He says the same to us, and we respond to that love by desire and suffering. And suffering is an admirable response—the best, I think. Try, then, to unite yourself with the supreme suffering whereby we were redeemed.

The Gift of Self

❧❧

THERE ARE SOULS WHO SEEK SOLITUDE merely in order to find themselves: there are others who seek it so that they may give themselves. Still, it remains to be lived!

Happy those who know how to put their whole soul into all they do. Because they are giving themselves, they will be able to bear much suffering, but their happiness will exceed their suffering, since the gift of self is the source and condition of life, and therefore of spiritual growth and joy. Go on, then, giving yourself: go on suffering . . . seek your joy in that precious suffering that the gift of self entails. God Who became man knew no more excellent way than this when He was on earth.

The Law of Contrasts

∽∽

GOD LOVES US, AND HIS USUAL WAY OF DEAL-
ing with souls is this. Wisely and lovingly He
apportions sweetness and bitterness, so that the
bitter shall prevent our growing enervated by
the sweet, and the sweet may help us to bear the
weight of the bitter. It is this law of contrasts which
is the normal cause of growth, and ends—and will
make us end, too—in final and perfect harmony.
It is also an infallible sign that God is dealing
mercifully with us. To be able to say *Thy Will
be done* immediately and calmly in the midst of
suffering—that is the perfection at which we must
aim. But God brings us to it by a road all must
follow. The rebellion of our nature, and the
struggles of our self-love, often make us advance,
provided we have the good will, far more than our
too rapid or too complete victories. These can
easily arouse spiritual pride or a false virtue which
is only on the surface. The long and bitter conflict
keeps us in our true place which is in impotence
and nothingness, and builds our soul upon foun-
dations that will never fail.

The Whole of our Human Nature is in the Will

∽∽

... *FIAT*. IN SUCH A DISPOSITION A SOUL can know hours of anguish, which Jesus called *even unto death*; but it has absolutely nothing to fear. Our whole moral life lies in the *Fiat voluntas Tua!* St Augustine declares: '*homines sunt voluntates*'— men are their wills! The whole of our human nature is in the will; the rest is just 'animal'. The hours when our lower nature rebels, these are the hours when it is dying. The bitter suffering comes from this death, and that is why it is both painful and necessary. The souls whom God plunges into this conflict are souls whom He loves; and when in the midst of it they say *Fiat* then it is they are souls that love. This *Fiat* places our will in line with the divine Will, and the two are made one. *He who cleaves to God becomes one spirit with Him.* To desire is to love: our desires are the measure of our hearts. They reveal the possibilities of union for each one of us; they are the moving in the depths of the soul of the Holy Spirit, Who is eternal Love. The struggle is the reconquest of that soul by Him Who is the life-giving Spirit against the forces of death which sin has left in us.

The Soul Places Itself in God's Will

ᔓᔕ

WHEN AFTER REFLECTION AND PRAYER WE place ourselves entirely in God's hands, we take the sole and most sure path to interior peace: that peace *which surpasseth all understanding*. For a soul that places itself in God's Will cannot be deceived. It shares in the very infallibility of God Himself. *In peace . . . I will sleep and will rest*. It is always possible that we may be troubled on the surface of our souls, and this superficial disturbance may well conceal our deeper peace, but we never really lose it. It is in these depths that we must take refuge when these moments of anguish come. There we find our true being, for there we find God from Whom we derive our being.

The Interior Life

ᔦᔧ

THE DISTURBANCES OF OUR SENSITIVE nature, provoked by suffering, or even joy, do not prove that we have no interior life. The interior life is not built up on insensibility, and can never be. Lack of sensitiveness is a defect, whereas sensitiveness is a very precious thing. Keep your sensitiveness keen, then, and try just simply to direct and control it. How? By subjecting it to reason, and to that higher reason which is our participation in the divine reason, namely faith.

But note well: I say, try to do this. That is, work hard to arrive at this goal. And in the meantime? . . . In the meantime, accept your weaknesses and offer them up to God, Who loves you. When we are weak, it is precisely in our weakness that God loves us, in order that He may communicate to us His strength. And when He has given us His strength, then He will love us as strong men.

Notice that this acceptance of our weakness is a great strength, because it is the most genuine form of humility. *He that shall humble himself shall be exalted.* We arise from our weakness when we say: 'My God, I accept it, and I offer it to you, because it is all I have. When you give me more, then I shall offer you more'.

The second thing is also very simple. Life on earth does not consist in being immune from conflict and danger, but in triumphing over them by grace.

We Must be Content

∾

WE MUST BE CONTENT WITH EVERYTHING—
even with being discontented! We must get right
out of ourselves, forget ourselves, so renounce ourselves that whether we are contented or discontented no longer matters, but only the good
pleasure of 'Him Who is'. God is not pleased by
our discontent, but He is by the vigour of soul we
display, the merits we acquire, and by the glory
we gain for Him when, instead of turning in upon
ourselves and brooding over our sufferings, we are
pleased because He is pleased. To love, after all,
is to give oneself, and to give oneself is to forget
oneself. *This do, and thou shalt live.*

Real Grace

∾∽

... IN ALL THESE TRIALS WE MUST RECOGNIZE the ever good and loving Will of God, and lovingly adore it. That is real grace. But only the Holy Spirit, present in the soul, can give this higher light. Enlightened by it, and by the *Fiat* it makes us utter, our spiritual misery becomes of no account: rather, the very means of our sanctification. Of it, as of all our troubles, we have only to say *Fiat voluntas Tua!* and it becomes clothed, like everything we offer to God, with His own goodness and majesty. How often have we not read this in St Paul and St Augustine. It is the very basis of their teaching as it is of the Gospel, because it is the very essence of God Himself, Who is Love. Our only trouble is that we are afraid to apply this teaching to ourselves. In our relations with God, the great—in fact, almost the only—fear we ought to have is of being afraid. We do not know how to reach the end of God's love—it has no end! Always see in Him a need to give Himself, for that is His very essence—Love, the gift of self. He cannot will or do otherwise.

This, then, is what God wants of us in our trials, and we acknowledge this when we say to Him: *Fiat voluntas Tua!* That is also why such a prayer covers the whole range of our failings and miseries.

Peace

〜〜

WE ALL, AT TIMES, SUFFER FROM GREAT illusions. We confuse not having peace with not being aware of the peace we possess. When our sensitive nature is all storm-tossed, we no longer perceive anything but the storm, because that occupies the most conscious part of ourselves. But that does not mean that we have lost our peace of soul, but only our awareness of it. All the same, that is enough to render these states extremely painful. This is our usual state in times of trial— an agitated sensitiveness, which makes us say: 'I have lost my interior peace'; when what we ought to say is: 'I am no longer conscious of it'.

We should get into the habit of believing in our peace of soul so long as we are not conscious of any grave fault. What is peace, after all, but *God present in the soul*? Provided, therefore, we have not offended Him gravely, God is there. To offend Him gravely, as you know, one must actually will to do so, and we haven't come to that yet.

The Real Secret of Interior Peace

∽∽

... THE REAL SECRET OF TRUE AND LASTING interior peace lies in detachment from the passing realities and events of life that go to make up its superficial pattern. All these things which are on the surface leave us empty and dissatisfied, even if they do not actually wound us. We need something else, and we turn instinctively to the only enduring reality here below—the inmost depth of our soul. For we have within us a kind of primal seed* from which our whole being with all its subsequent unfolding proceeds; and that tiny seed in its original essence never changes. It is this which assures the abiding continuity of our being, through all the incessant change that each day and hour bring. It is the continuous gift of Himself from Him Who is: and that gift partakes of His immensity and changelessness. When we detach ourselves from all that is passing and descend into these depths, we feel ourselves to be outside of all that is transitory and naught, and experience a peace which is His peace. *My peace I give unto you.*

Now Jesus has taught us that this place of intimacy is the kingdom of His Father: that He Who

*Translator's note: cf. 1 John iii. 9: *Semen ipsius (Dei) in eo manet . . . whosoever is born of God . . . His seed abideth in him.*

reigns there is not only 'Being that is' but 'Love Who gives Himself'. It is His own place apart, the bosom of the Father—*in sinu Patris*. And it is there He calls us: *Come to me, all you that labour and are burdened, and I will refresh you.* Refresh—in Latin: *re-ficiam*: I will make you anew. For there a continuous creation is taking place.

Perfect Love Casteth Out Fear

∽∾

NEVER FORGET THAT GOD IS LOVE, AND THAT the definition of any being indicates the limits of that being. Thus the 'limits' of God are infinite love: He is bound to love. His 'whole' is in love, and love's 'whole' is in Him. We have no right, therefore, to see anything but love in Him. Indeed, *There is no fear in love; but perfect love casteth out fear.* Dismiss altogether, then, from your thoughts this distressing fear, which died on the Cross— nay, even in the Crib. Keep up your heart, and rejoice in Him Who 'is', and is Love.

Action and Agitation

❧❧

WHERE WILL THIS LETTER FIND YOU, I wonder? It matters little. Our prayers, by way of God, know indeed how to reach you each day, and that suffices.

We strive to go out of this mortal frame of ours, which is bounded and limited by space. But however beautiful this frame may be, our soul, greater still, passes far, far beyond it to its own sphere, which is the infinite.

The whole trouble today is that we confuse action with agitation. Action and agitation are not only two different things; they are totally opposed. 'Nothing is so calm as living' was a saying of Gounod: and he believed it.

Try to rest more and more, then, in that detachment from all that is ephemeral, and in that union with the divine Will which is abiding.

Fear

∾∾

FEAR OF NOT RESPONDING SUFFICIENTLY TO
God's love is the sign of a faithful soul.

The Secret of our Peace of Soul

∽∽

FOR US, TIME AND SPACE ARE ONLY 'ACCI-dents' of a very poor reality. Our true life lies outside the uncertain limits that they impose on us. I still think of our happy conversation of some days ago, on the immutability of God. We should aim at the perfection itself of our heavenly Father, and endeavour to reflect, little by little, as far as possible, those traces of the divine Beauty which we call His attributes. That is the real basis and true Christian view of detachment. It is not really detachment, but an attachment. We leave the passing in order to enter into Him Who is eternal. There you have the secret of our peace of soul.

'I Will Sleep and I Will Rest'

∽∾

SOME THOUGHTS ARE EXPRESSED, OTHERS remain in the depths of the soul and will never find outward expression. This state of things may cause distress to a certain part of ourselves, but it accustoms us to live a higher form of life than can be described in words. This is true of a great number of our relations with God, even of the more essential and profound. St Augustine often speaks of the interior Master, Who instructs without words, and Whose teaching echoes in those sacred depths where everything lies engraved for eternity. Do not let us murmur, then, more than we can help, if in our mutual relations we are compelled by circumstances beyond our control to use this same language. And when it is a silence not of our own choosing, never think of it as a case of 'thou hast forsaken me'.

We have suffered, and we always shall, at finding that what the world offers us is only too often an appearance, a counterfeit reality. Healthy anguish! Hearts too easily contented in this life will not perhaps be so hereafter. The world is bound to leave a great void in our hearts—a void that only God can fill. Ask Him to fill it more and more.

'Thou has made us for Thyself, and our hearts are restless until they rest in Thee'. We shall have our rest one day, in the very measure of our sufferings in this life. Let us rest even now. Rest in God's goodness. *In peace . . . I will sleep and I will rest.* I strongly recommend you to ponder over those two words: *sleep* and *rest*. It is not for nothing that the Holy Spirit has linked them together. There is, as you know, a sleep which is no repose. There is, on the other hand, a sleep which gives rest to our whole being.

Sleep in God—the sleep of a soul which puts all its cares and anxieties entirely into His hands: this is the sleep which is true repose.

Requiescat in Pace

∽∽

'THERE HAS JUST DIED OUR VENERABLE sister in Christ . . . professed choir Sister of our convent of Holy Cross at Beauregard. She died here, at our convent of San Francesco, of which she was formerly Prioress, in the ninety-second year of her age, and the sixty-fourth of her religious profession. May she rest in peace!'

Such is the announcement of her death as we have sent it to the different houses of the Order, so that all may pray for the repose of her soul. During the sixty-six years of her Carthusian life this brave soul had been a model religious, and the serenity of her passing has filled the house with its fragrance. I thought of you as I listened to the well-loved bell tolling for her. It seemed to be doing its best to give out a sound of sadness, but in spite of everything it filled our souls with joy.

Flowers of Paradise

❦

... THESE THOUGHTS ARE OURS, AND THEY
are dear to us. And they are ours, because they are
dear to us. The more we love them, the more they
become part of ourselves. These are the flowers of
Paradise in our souls, but flowers that blossomed
first in the Garden of the Agony. Cherish them,
and give them the setting of our sufferings resting
in our love for Him: a bouquet, indeed, worthy of
the place of honour. But better still, put them
in the hidden chamber where *the Father seeth in
secret.*

God is Love

∽∾

... BELIEVE MORE AND MORE INTENSELY IN
God's love. Or, better, that God *is* Love: that, for
Him, to be and to love are one and the same thing.
Remember what St Augustine wrote on the text:
'I am, Who am'. Change the word 'being' for
'loving' and you will still be far from reaching the
limits of that Truth which is Love. Despite all
the penetration of his genius St Augustine never
reached those limits. No one ever will—there are
no limits! The Love of God is boundless Light.

Knowledge and Love

∽∾

HERE, I THINK, IS THE PRECISE POINT WHERE we disagree. For you, knowledge which is the result of human effort (even when that effort is inspired by the purest love) is the condition of love, and therefore of sanctity. But it is not so at all. For such knowledge is the fruit of genius, which counts for nothing in the light of eternity. The love which urged the great mind of St Augustine to search to know more and more of God, the object of his love, and the love which inspired the Curé of Ars towards the same end, are not differentiated by the degree of intellectual penetration to which they attained, but by a certain initial impulse which was the stirring of the Holy Spirit within them. In which was this stirring stronger? We do not know. Only the divine moving power, the Holy Spirit Himself, can answer that question.

Sanctity, in other words, is not the outcome of intellectual effort, nor the result of intellectual gifts, but is union with Truth—a union which is constantly urging us to an ever deeper knowledge of God. And this union with Truth is the work, not of knowledge but of love. So your axiom that 'of two saints, it is the one who knows most that loves most and is the holier' should be reversed. What should say is: 'of two saints, it is the one who loves most that knows most'. But this knowledge is not a knowledge of genius, but of the Holy Spirit. They are two different kinds of knowledge.

But, apart from this, I make no difficulty in admitting that St Augustine possessed both kinds in an eminent degree.

St Augustine

⊷⊷

THIS IS THE SECRET OF THE TREMENDOUS
influence of St Augustine.

If his mind, which was certainly amazing, had
not been completely pervaded and, as it were,
moulded through and through by the qualities of
his heart; if his thought had not been deep with
love; if he had not loved what he thought and in
the measure of his thought—if these two faculties
had not been so finely balanced and fused . . . he
would have been forgotten long ago, or known
only to scholars. Anyway, he would not be St
Augustine!

Genius and Sanctity

∽∾

YOU WANT TO ENDOW GENIUS WITH A SPECIAL love of God, arising out of its specially penetrating knowledge of Him. But this special penetration, and the particular love which proceeds from it, are the fruit of genius, but genius moved by the Holy Spirit. Genius, as genius, would then condition the development of the Spirit of Love in a soul, and consequently its sanctity.

I think one can and should concede that much. One must only be on one's guard against attributing to genius a causality which it does not possess. It is an instrumental cause, but it is not the principal cause. The principal cause remains the Holy Spirit, the Spirit of Love, Who seizes upon this force and brings it within the sweep of His sanctifying action, just as He uses health, physical strength, the happy balance of one's constitution, external influences, the environment in which one lives—all favourable conditions, but not causes.

It seems to me that expressed in these terms and in this form, the question becomes a simple one. Divine Love, the sole moving power, takes St Augustine with his temperament and genius, his country and heredity, with his father's hot blood and his mother's deep, ardent soul; with his own need to know and to love; with his teachers and his friends—all these things—and harmoniously guides this whole towards his soul's final union with God. It is obvious that if such, and so rich, a whole allows itself to be led, the results will be incomparable. Such is the rôle of genius in the work of sanctity—a precious instrument in the hands of Divine Love. It serves Love's purposes, but it does not effect them. Divine Love can do without it, and can accomplish even greater and better things without this instrument, if He so will. He has done so more than once. He has given souls who lacked intellectual gifts marvellous intuitions, and, along with them, a love equal or even greater in proportion.

We Must Love Even the Desire to Love

〰〰

... IT IS BECAUSE GOD IS THE CENTRE WHERE our souls meet that the hours when we speak together of Him are so dear to us. And how quickly they pass! Your conversations remind me of Pascal's saying: 'You would not seek me, had you not already found me'. To want to love is already to love. *My soul hath coveted to long for thy justifications.* One must love even this desire. We suffer from this desire, but we ought not to, really. It is the best part of our soul, and has its origin in its extreme depths—in those depths which nothing created can fill, and which cry out for God. There, deep within us, God is present, but we do not comprehend His presence sufficiently, and we are too anxious to do so, or rather to feel it. We would like to perceive Him as we perceive a flower, or as we grasp some great truth. But God is altogether different, and our relations with Him are of an entirely different nature. In one of the finest passages in his *Confessions* St Augustine passes in review the whole of creation, and implores all creatures to tell him: 'Where is God, and what is he?' And all make answer: 'You must seek higher'. Our knowledge of God amounts very much to this: that He is greater than all His works, and that to possess Him we must pass beyond them all.

Do not be surprised, then, if His presence in the depths of the soul does not make itself felt as in the case of created things. It is precisely the distinguishing sign of His action that He gives Himself to us under a form essentially hidden and incomprehensible. To 'perceive' God, we need the higher faculty of inward vision, the inner light. Pray, then, that this inner light may grow. For that we must use it, but use it in peace—a peace which comes to us through trust.

Life is a Unity

∽∽

'I AM SO MANY YEARS OF AGE'. WHAT DOES such a statement mean? It means only this: that the earth has gone round the sun so many times since I came into the world. That is the normal measure of what the world calls time. But there is another 'age' which consists in interior movement and progress proper to each individual, as opposed to periodic movements which are from without, and are the same for all.

Our real age depends upon the interior events which have taken place within the soul, upon their rhythm, and upon the greatly varying reactions, entirely personal and unique, resulting from them. That is our true age, and it is an age which varies with each individual. There are old men who are not really more than twenty years of age, whilst there are young men who are in reality old. But this is only the superficial side of the question. There is another side, the moral side, which interests us much more.

Life is a unity: and that unity is the fruit of a certain order, just as that order is itself the fruit of subordination or submission. We can only be said to 'live' when our sensitive nature submits itself to reason, our body to the soul. Perfect life implies perfect subordination—every act of volition on the part of the spirit is at once consented to and accepted by the lower part of our nature; and when our reason is itself truly subject to God, then you have perfect order and fullness of life. The more, on the other hand, these elements are in opposition, the more our being is disintegrated, and the more our true life suffers.

You tell me: 'I find in myself tendencies which I cannot control'. I reply: 'That is a lack of order'. You add: 'I suffer because this is so, and I would like to achieve submission and order'. Again I reply: 'Accept this suffering: that acceptance alone will bring order, until such time as you can achieve it directly in the co-ordinated harmony of your faculties under control'.

Here we touch on a very deep principle. Plato expressed it when he said: 'When we break away from order through some fault, we can only return to order through suffering'. Again, this is the basis of the Gospel and of the teaching of St Paul, from which St Augustine received his inspiration.

Spiritual Time

〰〰

... OUR LIFE IN GOD IS, IN FACT, A PARTICI-
pation in all His perfections—His immutability,
His eternity. None the less, as long as time lasts—
because we are still in the body—we must in a
certain sense and to a certain degree remain subject to the rule of successive duration. The era of
eternal duration will only reach its plenitude when
the soul has re-assumed its body. But this re-
assumption will not involve any change, properly
speaking, except for the body, which will then
enter into a new state. The soul itself does not
change, any more than God does when He creates.

All these questions are extremely difficult, since
the realities under discussion are so utterly different from those to which we are accustomed. Spiritual time is not the same as our time: it measures,
not the motion of matter but the activity of the
spirit.

One instant of such time is an act of the spirit.
These instants need not be linked together as ours
are. But it is impossible for us to grasp these things
clearly, because we have no adequate terms of
comparison. Life is simple, and the truer and
higher it is, the simpler it becomes. But the science
of life is extremely complicated.

'Thou Shalt Sprinkle Me with Hyssop'

✌

UNDER THE OLD LAW, LEPERS WERE HEALED BY being sprinkled with the blood of the sacrifices on a tiny bunch of hyssop. Hyssop, the little rock plant, represented the humility of Christ, the shedding of Whose Blood would one day cleanse the leprosy of our souls.

In using hyssop to purify his sinful soul, David thus acknowledged his sin, and humbled himself because of it. His humility united him to the humble Saviour in Whom he placed his trust. And in that union, our Saviour communicates His Blood to him, touches his wounds with It, causes It to flow through his very veins, and so restores him to a purity which is His very own—the divine purity, purer far than any earthly purity: the immaculate whiteness of Him Whom the Fathers of the Church call 'the First Virgin'; and of which the radiance even of snow is but a distant and, as it were, frigid image. *Thou shalt wash me, and I shall be made whiter than snow.*

Notice that David the sinner does not sprinkle himself with hyssop; he does not purify himself— only God can do that. The work of regeneration is not ours, but the work of the Holy Spirit within us. *Restore unto me the joy of Thy salvation . . . O God, the God of my salvation . . . O Lord, open Thou*

70

my lips . . . Deal favourably in Thy good will. You see from this how groundless our fears are, and above all how lacking in understanding. For there, by the divine Light, we see revealed a Being Who is Love—that is, the gift of self: One Who is longing to give Himself infinitely; Whose whole Being is, as it were, unceasingly inclined towards us, in order that He may pour Himself into us. All that He is waiting for is the emptiness of our souls to welcome the outpouring of His fullness. Hence, what He seeks are souls with the courage and the understanding to say: 'Miserere—have mercy. Dear Lord, you see my wretched state: fill me with your Being, which is wealth beyond all telling'. That first word uttered, the rest will follow unfailingly—*that the walls of Jerusalem may be built up.*

But the sacrifice of justice and of burnt-offerings must be made *upon Thine altar*—that is, in the union of the surrendered soul, which by its immolation is lifted up . . . even unto God.

The Master's Plan

෴

IT IS NOT A QUESTION OF LOVING WHAT IS EVIL or painful, but of suffering it in order either to set it right or bring it to an end. That is God's way. He doesn't love evil, but He permits it for the sake of the good He draws out of it. Evil, like all reality, is a marvellous instrument in the hands of divine Providence. We shall be amazed one day—in the next world—to see what suffering will have accomplished in courageous souls, who know how to accept it and bear it out of love. It is the deepest source of true peace.

No one wants us to suffer, but we should love suffering as God loves it—that is, as something uplifting and a harbinger of peace. The world is made according to a plan which we cannot alter: it is the Master's plan. We are only servants, and we must take life as He has planned it, and bring our wills and efforts into conformity with His designs.

Now suffering falls within this plan. It is the way to joy, just as death—or mortification, which is death to self—is the way to life. *He that shall lose his life . . . shall find it.* We are tiny seeds cast into the ground, and we must die if we would live anew in God. There are some verses in the 125th Psalm which give a wonderful picture of this divine plan;

but it is not enough merely to submit to it as to something inevitable; we must love it as an expression of divine love.

For that we must be strong. But being strong does not mean resisting what is wounding us to rid ourselves of it. There is another, and much higher, kind of strength. It is that strength which accepts what it cannot get rid of, remaining all the while smiling under the cross. It is not to the cross we smile, but to Him Who carried it before us and for us, and Who carries it with us still.

We Must Accept this Divine Plan

∽∽

O UR SUFFERING OUGHT NOT REALLY TO UPSET us. It is a state almost necessary for those souls for whom this world is too small. They need breathing space, and this world stifles them. Suffering betrays that longing for God in every part of us that remains unsatisfied with itself. So don't mind suffering greatly from this very suffering: God will never lay it to our charge. Try to remain calm, and very still. For this God for Whom we are longing in our hearts has loved us from the beginning, and will love us to the end. There is nothing He wants more than to give Himself to us, and the greatest joy we can give Him is to believe this.

Deep in our hearts we believe this, but we are too anxious to feel and enjoy this faith. There is the danger; nay, indeed, it is the mistake we make. To believe in God is one thing; to 'taste and see how sweet' He is, is quite another. God never refuses the former to us if our will is good, but the latter depends entirely upon His good will and pleasure. The one is the gift we make to Him of our mind, the other is a communication of His own joy which He makes to us.

Now we should—and can—make this gift of our mind to His Mind; but to share in His joy in this life as we would like to, is not within our power.

74

The most we can do is to be thankful for the temporary first-fruits and foretastes that He is pleased to give us from time to time, as and when He wills. We must accept this divine plan, which reserves for another world the final and full possession of the object of our love. This world is, and always will be, a place of exile and pilgrimage; a desert to be crossed, where for a moment we pitch our tent, soon to strike it again and continue our journey. We so quickly forget this, and as we make our way we do not keep our eyes fixed sufficiently on that Promised Land, where our true happiness lies.*

Translator's note: cf. the Collect for the IV Sunday after Easter: . . . *ibi nostra fixa sint corda, ubi vera sunt gaudia.*

Why We Must Suffer

໖໖

IN THE DIVINE PLAN, THERE IS BUT ONE MAN—
Ecce Homo; but one truth, one way, one life. *Ego
sum via, veritas et vita ... I am the Way,
the Truth and the Life.* Everyman, loved by God,
must become one with that Man, know that
Truth, follow that Way, and enter into that
Life.

To give that supreme grace to each one of us,
God stops at nothing. There are times when He
will turn the whole world upside-down if thereby
one single soul may come to resemble His divine
Son more. That is all He wants, that is all He
can want: the whole plan of divine Providence is
directed to that end. All that happens to us must
be regarded in the great light of this final end. That
is why we all suffer—to become 'other Christs'; to
be Jesus over again, and, like Him, misunderstood,
persecuted, and made to bear our cross. Looked
at from any other point of view, suffering would
be incomprehensible and intolerable. On the other
hand, when we contemplate our divine Example—
He, the Truth and the Life—suffering assumes a
beauty which is the loveliest thing God has permitted here below, just as death is the most living of
the realities of this life.

To find joy in sorrow, life in death—that is the

great secret by which our wounds are healed . . .
but you won't find it in any of your text-books!

Providential Bitterness

∽∾

EXPERIENCE TEACHES US TO KNOW LIFE AND
men, and we are forced to the conclusion that if
there is nothing beyond what this world offers to
satisfy our craving for infinite happiness, then life
is indeed a very poor affair, and we shall never be
satisfied. It is good to have experienced this, to
have had first-hand, living contact with it. What
books tell us about it is not worth one instant of
personal experience, and these moments in our
lives are not lost; far from it! They are treasures
for time, and, if we accept them in a spirit of
faith, for eternity too. And they are precious graces
also, for they keep us detached, and that is not so
easy. Despite the bitterness of the many disil-
lusionments in life, we allow ourselves to be so
easily drawn away by transitory things. Fortunately
for us, God has diffused a kind of providential
bitterness over all created things, which turns us
away from them, or, better still, holds them off
from us.

We shall thank Him one day for these marks of
His love, but we cannot expect either to understand them or to appreciate them in this life.

Our Griefs

EVERY GREAT GRIEF CONCEALS A GREAT grace. God does for us exactly what we ourselves would do, if need be, for our own children. He inflicts pain in order to cure. Or, more correctly, He does not cause, He permits, the pain (which He does not want), in order to ensure the cure, which is His sole will.

God is Behind Everything

∽∾

WE ARE BETTER THAN WE THINK . . . AND SO ARE others! There is a golden mean, not at all easy to find, between optimism (which sees only the good in things) and pessimism (which sees only the bad). There is good and bad in all the material God uses. The bad is more apparent, because it is on the surface; but it is the good which will prevail in the end. Whenever one has occasion to speak at all intimately with others, one is always favourably surprised: they are so much better than one thought! Believe, then, in the good in ourselves and in others; that is how God looks at things. The world was frighteningly evil when Jesus came into it—but it didn't stop Him coming . . .

The first thing, then, is not to be afraid, either of ourselves or of others. We must face life. It is this deep and prolonged contemplation of reality which brings us to God, for He is behind everything. Everything *is* because He has either willed it or permitted it. And if the evil permitted by Him frightens us, we must say to ourselves that underneath it all is some good, and that it is this good that God wills. I can say, therefore, that even when I contemplate the evil, there is something of God's Will (and therefore of His Love) hidden at the root of everything.

It is this Will (or this Love) that we seek, and we suffer from not finding it as much as we would like—a noble form of suffering, indeed. Thank God for having placed it deep in our hearts—a cry, as it were, from Him to us, and an answering cry from us to Him. But be consoled: there is a remedy for our anguish, and that is true faith. I say, true: for there is a kind of faith which adheres to truth solely with the mind, and another which adheres with the heart. The first is not enough: it is cold and distant, it doesn't unite; it leaves us far from God and empty. The second kind more than fills us, since it effects union. This true and living faith is like a taking possession of God: He becomes ours; He becomes the soul's beloved Guest. And that soul, detached from earthly things, has only to turn to Him by a loving thought to realize that at last it has reached that intimacy of which it has dreamed.

That is where, I think, God is calling us. But we arrive there only after a long journey, which takes us away from ourselves and from creatures. But we shall have the courage to stay this long and hard course, and we shall know the joy of having reached our goal.

God is Love

∽∾

WE CAN NEVER BE URGED TOO STRONGLY TO meditate upon the definition that God has given of Himself: *Deus est Caritas . . . God is Love*. There we shall find the answer to all our doubts, and a source of consolation in all our troubles. We know only too well the selfishness that is paramount in the world. The number of those who know how to give themselves (and want to do so) is not legion. This is because our 'being' is so limited, and consequently we have so little to give. And amongst those who seem to give themselves, many are simply giving themselves to themselves: in other words, they are not giving themselves at all. They are only seeking something in others to complete themselves; not that they may complete others. It is in this respect that God is so infinitely superior to us, for He is Love—the gift of self. He is overflowing Plenitude, yearning to pour Himself out into our nothingness, in order that He may fill it with His infinite Being. To give Himself, therefore, is 'being' to Him, as well as His life and joy. The weaker and emptier we are, and the more helpless and imperfect, the greater is the capacity He finds in us to receive Him. Love, then, for us consists above all in accepting this outpouring of life; for Him, love consists in bestowing it.

82

It is this love which is at the root of everything . . . but it wants finding! God has given us a light, however, to help us to discover it, and this light we call the light of faith. Now faith is a participation in God's own light. The faithful soul sees in everything—in men, things and events—what God sees in them: it sees them in His spirit of love, which is communicated to that soul. In a word, it sees only that Love, giving Himself in everything—*Deus Caritas*.

Life is a Question of Faith and Will

~∾~

FOR REASONS KNOWN ONLY TO HIMSELF, AND which always have their origin in His love, God does not necessarily let us 'taste' peace. But that does not mean that we haven't it. We must distinguish clearly between the feeling of possession, and the actual possession of God. There are countless souls who possess God, who derive no pleasure from that fact. The perception of our possession of God is a very lovely thing, but it isn't necessary. Life is a question of faith and will. We must believe that God loves us, and that, provided no grave fault has driven His sacred presence from our soul, He is there, living and giving Himself. And that life of God within us is at the same time our life in Him. If we do what He tells us, and respond as far as we can to all He asks of us, our love for Him will be genuine. If we fall—well, we must get up again, and at once resume our friendship with Him, as He at once does with us. All religion consists in that. If He adds feelings of interior joy, so much the better; but if we feel nothing, it doesn't matter . . . our soul is quite safe, and we are living as God wants us to.

We should continue, then, to give ourselves without stint or reserve, whether we pray or work—in fraternal charity, in excusing the faults

of others, with an entire forgetfulness of self, and
in boundless confidence in God's love.

God's Power is His Love

∽∾∽

NEVER FORGET THAT GOD'S POWER IS HIS love, and that our misery is no obstacle to that love. On the contrary, St Francis of Sales affirms that our need serves as a kind of throne for Divine Love. We think too much about our own wretched selves, and that is why we are so unhappy. The beautiful saying of St Augustine is well known: 'We are made for God, and our heart remains restless and troubled until it finds rest in him'. Ask Him to teach us to live this truth. In practice, this is how it should be lived . . . It is not a question, as you may well imagine, of getting rid of all our faults and failures, but of turning to God with these very faults and failings, and of giving ourselves to Him just as we are. How many souls would enjoy divine peace, if only they realized this and acted on it. We spend our time bemoaning our faults and looking at ourselves, instead of looking at Him and growing greater. For that is what He is—Infinite Love, longing for us to give ourselves to Him so that He may give Himself to us.

This comes from the false idea we have of Him. We think of Him in terms of our own littleness, and judge His love by our own. But God is so infinitely removed from all this. His majesty, His joy, His beauty and life consist of the gift of Himself, for He is Love. He awaits but one word from us, and it is this: *Et nos credidimus Caritati . . . we have believed in His love.* By these words we 'take possession' of Him; almost as though we actually held Him. They create a bond between us which makes Him ours, so that henceforth we can say: 'My God'.

But again, this *credidimus*—we have believed— means that we trust Him; that we surrender ourselves, give ourselves to Him. It is our love giving itself to Infinite Love, whereby the two are made one.

We must not be afraid to look at things in this light and to direct our lives accordingly. All we need is good will and grace (which is God's good will): the two forces that make saints. Let us, then, resolutely put aside our fears, and throw ourselves joyfully into that filial confidence which is the first and last word of the Gospel. You must not think of yourself as carrying a lonely burden of existence and life. There could not be a more fatal mistake. God is offering Himself to us in order that He may fill our soul's loneliness and turn our desolation into joy. The desolation is on the shifting surface of the soul, where the devil loves to make trouble, whereas the joy is the real and substantial depth where God is giving Himself . . . *Enter thou into the joy of thy Lord.*

The Great Reality

〜〜

WE WANT GOD, AND SO WE LOVE HIM; AND WE know the consequences and the conclusion. (I am not inventing this, I am simply quoting Our Lord's own words). *If any man love me . . . my Father will love him, and we will come to him, and will make our abode with him.* We love Him, and He, Divine Love, draws into us the very presence of the three divine Persons.

We do not think enough of this, and when we do we so soon forget it. This is the great reality, which should hold the whole of our attention; and it is in the light of this truth that we should look at and appraise everything here below. It has always been our conviction that God was calling us to live this truth with a particular intensity. Perhaps that is why, almost unknown to ourselves, we have always felt the utter insufficiency of creatures, and the transitoriness of this life. The deep interior anguish which results from this conviction is reserved for those souls whom God is calling to a higher life. God keeps them almost continually aware of the sheer nothingness of all that is around them, in order to detach them from it, so that He may take possession of them more readily. Such souls suffer terribly—and from practically everything. But the soul's interior citadel is enriched by this suffering, which creates a deep gulf between it and the world.

God's Paternal Love

໌ผผ

A MOTHER'S LOVE, DEEP THOUGH IT CAN BE, IS but an infinitesimal drop in the ocean of the charity and paternal love of God for the souls of every one of us. And the tender joy we experience when we surrender ourselves to her love and love her in return, is nothing more than a distant and totally inadequate image of the joy God has in store for those who are prepared to accept His love and respond to it.

Strength of Soul

✐

STRENGTH OF SOUL DOES NOT MEAN LACK OF feeling. It is not unfeeling souls that are strong. Strength of soul consists in rising above suffering, in bearing it bravely, in setting before ourselves the highest motives for living, and in allowing ourselves to be guided by them. Of these motives, the highest and most powerful are the supernatural; in other words, the thought of God Who alone can satisfy our hearts, and Who offers Himself to us for that very purpose. But there are also natural motives, which we must not overlook.

A man who is at the mercy of his trials and of his feelings is not fulfilling the end God has in view for him. He is growing smaller, and is no longer worthy of being called a man. Time passes with him, but more or less aimlessly. He plays no part in the world, and does no good. He hasn't the influence he might have. Humanly speaking, and from a supernatural point of view, he is useless and a failure.

∽∾

THE GRACES WITH WHICH GOD HAS SO PLENTI-
fully endowed our soul and by which He has sur-
rounded our very existence, reveal His designs in
our regard. Life should be the most perfect realization possible of those designs. So often we do
not realize them because we do not comprehend
them sufficiently, and this because we are so occupied with ourselves, with our own 'self'.

This 'self' as we call it, in our spiritual life, is
not our true and whole being; it is only a part,
and the tiniest and least interesting part. This
false and inferior self consists in the series of unim-
portant happenings which go to make up life, considered in themselves. It is the sorrow that
'endureth for a night' and the joy that 'cometh
with the morning'; it is our age, the cut of our
figure, our health, our success, our reputation—
the reactions of our sensitive nature in the face of
all these transitory things. Our true and whole self
are these same circumstances, but viewed as part
of the plan of Divine Love, and contributing to its
realization. We are too much taken up with the
first 'self', and when we suffer, we brood over our
suffering, forgetting that this suffering can be the
very means of supernatural joy in us. We appraise
everything—persons, things and events—from the

human point of view, which is so ephemeral and narrow. Our values should be God's eternal values. Then things would open out and become beautiful. It is this life of faith which is the very life of God within us. Then it is not 'we' who live, but the Eternal Father Who 'sends the Paraclete' to us, by Whose life we live.

The early Christians saturated their minds with these truths, which are so forgotten in these days. It was the secret of their strength, and it must become ours. Where is the world tending? The days are dark, and the spirit of evil is at work in the world just now. There will be no victory save for those in whom the Spirit of God reigns. Let us keep closely united in that Spirit, Who is infinite Love.

True Life

～～

IF ONLY WE REALIZED HOW WE COMPLICATE
life, when in reality it is so simple. All our troubles
come from this: that we do not know how to seek
God where He is. We seek Him far away, and all
the while He is quite close to us. *In Him we live,
and move and have our being*. This is true from
the natural point of view, but above all from the
supernatural. God is the soul of our soul: that is,
the Principle that gives it life. It is *there* that we
must seek Him, and it is there we shall find Him
'without end'. That is what the saints did. They
kept themselves *ante faciem Dei viventis . . . before
the face of the living God*. And God, thus contem-
plated by an interior regard, communicated Himself to them and lived in them. They saw Him, and
their 'seeing' was a participation in the eternal
knowledge He has of Himself. He was 'born again'
in them—that Word, which was a reflection or
image of the Eternal Father and of their own souls.
Truly, then, can we say that the divine life was
generated in them, and became their life.

And it can be so with us, even in our busiest
moments. It is not necessary to seek the stillness
of a sanctuary or of our *prie-Dieu*. All we need to
do is to make an act of faith and love: 'My God,
I believe in you, and I love you': a simple move-

94

ment in the depths of our soul that we call forth from time to time. This is true life.

To Believe is to See Things in God's Light

❦

THE FUTURE DOES NOT REST WITH US. IT IS not what we make of it, for God alone has the planning of it. The most we can do is to accept trustingly His divine action, which is the expression of His love. We must not think so much about people, and things and events: that side of life is so often depressing. We should look rather at Him Who with kingly power controls these shifting scenes, making them fit in according to the plan of His infinite love. We should steep ourselves more and more in this spirit of faith, which alone is reasonable and true. That is how God sees things. In all He does or permits, He sees and desires only His own love, and that is what we should see and desire too.

It is quite true that the world seems in a very bad way. It is full of evil and hatred. How can we see love, where everything points the other way? We do not see it: we believe it. To believe is to see things in God's light; to leave everything to Him Who says: 'Your bodily eyes and your reason see only evil, but this is superficial. At the bottom of everything is Love . . . Believe My word'. Faith does, indeed, call for a very big sacrifice, but this same faith gives us a sense of security and peace, which might almost be called infinite, so surely does it rest on the word of God Himself. Here we have the profound secret of Christian serenity in the midst of the most painful trials, which are only passing, whereas the word of God is something eternal.

Sons of Joy

ᔕᔐ

TRY MORE AND MORE TO TURN YOUR MIND away from its sad thoughts. Sadness, in principle, cannot come from God, for He is joy. And even when He permits these times of trial, it is that we may find His joy through the trial. His own great joy is to give Himself, for He is Love. And we should enter into that joy. *Intra in gaudium Domini tui . . . enter thou into the joy of thy Lord.* We enter into it by believing in His love, whilst faith makes contact with Him, and enables Him to give Himself. Our joy is to believe that we are loved by Someone Who is Infinite Love. *In caritate perpetua dilexi te, et ideo attraxi te . . . I have loved thee with an everlasting love, therefore have I drawn thee.* We feel strongly drawn to God, because of His great love for us. How sad it is that this reality, which is the only true and ultimate reality, is not more familiar to us, more intimately real. It would infuse joy into even the most painful trials, and bring peace and contentment to those deep parts of the soul where, in the hours of its greatest anguish, we would find a place of shelter and repose.

We are sons of joy, because we are children of God.

Lawful Affections

༄ྃ

PEACE IS, AS IT WERE, THE ATMOSPHERE OF THE soul seeking God, which needs to feel peace if it is to follow the hard road that leads to Him. But this peace comes, not because the soul feels brave and strong, but because it is leaning on Him Who is *Deus fortis . . . God the Mighty*, the God of Love. The soul, having the conviction of this support, fears nothing, and cannot fear. Or, if it does, its fears are no more than passing impressions, which it throws off quickly, placing them in the heart of that infinite Charity, which transmutes fear into confidence and love.

It is in this all-embracing plan of Divine Love that our affections become lawful and a source of sanctification. One might almost say that they are necessary. The Heart of Jesus was anything but unfeeling. We know how deeply He loved His Mother and St John, and the family at Bethany . . . But His affections were controlled and directed, and when, one after the other, He had to leave all these to whom He had given His love so unreservedly, He pronounced His *Fiat*, and this in itself was a still further expression of His love and of the gift of Himself.

God means us to have family affections. Not only are they good, but they create ties which ennoble our being by linking us up with those who have gone before us, and with those who are to come after. We are not isolated beings; we form an immense family in Eternal Love, in Whom we must all be united. Individual families are the links in this immense family, and we should all be welded together in divine Charity.

These family affections are a grace, and a safeguard for us in this life, as well as proof of the integrity of a soul which has known how to keep its innocence. They serve, moreover, to raise us up to Him Who wants us to call Him *Our Father*. We should accustom ourselves to pass almost naturally from one to the other; or, better still, to see one in the other. Our earthly father is the living and visible image of our heavenly Father, Whose love we see reflected in him. The life of faith thus enables us to supernaturalize all these realities innate in us. It is the Holy Spirit communicating His own light to us, so that we may see what He sees. He joins Himself to our spirit so that we can penetrate that higher world, from which we came and to which we must return.

Natural Affection

～～

WE ARE NOT STRAYING IN ANY WAY FROM GOD by loving our father or our country. On the contrary, we would be going against His Will if we acted otherwise. We mustn't think, then, either of suppressing or of limiting this affection, but simply of directing it. Above our earthly father is our heavenly Father, and they are not in opposition but are subordinated the one to the other. So our love for them must be a unitive force, which sees the one in the other; the one as the image and likeness of the other. Thus considered, natural affection, far from disappearing altogether, becomes greater, since it is now one with God's love. Rest assured that God Himself will guide and support us by helping us thus to introduce a unity into our affections. It is such a big mistake to think that He wants to crush out our natural feelings; He does not: He fosters them more and more by giving them satisfaction which is infinite.

In this perfect harmony, then, of our soul and our life with the divine Will, we shall be ever ready to respond to more precise demands, should He make them known to us.

Light in Which We Find Peace

❧

G OD SO ARRANGES THINGS THAT WE ALL HAVE some days of greater recollection, and these days do us untold good, and are most precious. Even in religion, where our walls shut out the world so completely, we need them. The ordinary routine of life saps the energies of the soul, and the spring of our spirit would gradually become slack were it not rewound from time to time. This is one of the weaknesses of our nature, and it is as well to know it and admit it. It reveals us in our true light, and we understand better the wretchedness of our poor nature, weakened by original sin.

But we must not be disheartened when we see ourselves constantly slipping on the downward path which leads to our nothingness, for Jesus came to teach us how to climb back again up this path, and we realize all the more how grateful we should be to our divine Redeemer, Who came to restore us. It is in this light of our divine redemption that we shall, more and more, find peace and joy. *Omnia possum in eo qui me confortat . . . I can do all things in Him Who strengtheneth me.* Confidence in God creates in our souls a kind of sacred retreat, where we find shelter and refuge from the buffetings of life. Nothing can touch us there: even the greatest trials are always from something created and consequently finite and transitory; whereas Jesus is ever the Uncreated, the Changeless and the Infinite.

The mistake we make, and the source of all our hours of anguish, comes from our wanting the feeling of peace to be our only feeling. But that is not God's plan. In His infinitely wise love, He has foreseen that a world in which peace and anxiety, joy and sorrow, good and evil, intermingle, will better procure His glory, which is His ultimate end. This plan is good, because it is His plan; and placing all our faith in its goodness we partake in some measure in Him Who is its Source and Witness. Then we see things from quite a different angle, infinitely simple and consoling. I say we see: not that we understand. It is not necessary to understand. To understand is an act of the mind, which gives us satisfaction as does the exercise of all activity that we can call our own. To believe is an act which draws us into the activity of Him in Whom we believe; and when He in Whom we believe is Infinite Wisdom, to believe is to participate in that Wisdom, and is therefore infinitely wise.

That is why, for us, prayer and faith are such a stronghold against everything.

The Great Secret of our Peace

∾∾

WE HAVE NOT LOST OUR PEACE OF SOUL; ONLY the surface has been troubled. But we are so accustomed to live on the surface that these superficial storms make us think that the depths are troubled too. But these things are necessary and do us good, for they teach us to live in those depths, and force us to love (and to desire and seek) the large serenity of those souls who know that God is All; that He loves our souls, and that our very sufferings and trials become a means of union with His love. We learn in these same hours the need to live united with Him, and we realize that this union does not take place in the realm of our feelings (since God is essentially a spirit), but in the depths of our spiritual will, which we neither see nor feel, and that it is none the less true and substantial love.

We must never be surprised at any 'badness' either in others or in ourselves, but always see over and against the badness the infinite goodness of Him Who came to heal us. See all this in the divine plan. God could have willed a humanity without any failings or evil. But it is not a question of what He could have willed and done, but of what He actually has willed and done. The great secret of our peace lies in the acceptance of that

Will, but we have to learn to make that acceptance just as we have to learn everything in this life. Wicked people are instruments in the hands of divine Providence: they oblige us to face trying decisions and acts of the will. Faith has not taken root until it has had to struggle to say: 'My God, I adore your hand and your love in this person who is doing me an injustice, and in that temperament which jars on me'. Faith is the light which reveals God under the veil of creatures, but it has to be a very living faith to see Him through some of them! Yet He is always there. Jesus, on the Cross, did not say: 'How weak and evil men are', but: *Father, forgive them . . .* And again: *Father, into thy hands I commend my spirit.* Life is completely changed when, no matter the circumstances but especially in moments of great agony, we are able to say: *Father.* However, such faith is very rare. As a rule, we see only the suffering, its cause and instruments, the means of getting rid of it, and so on . . . But when we ourselves have suffered, we begin to understand not only how much Jesus suffered (and that is already very important), but how in His suffering His gaze went far beyond the suffering and saw only the Father Whom it was glorifying. One realizes also how difficult it is to forget oneself, and to arrive at that supreme gift of self, which was our salvation.

The Liberty of the Children of God

∽∾

OUR SERENITY OF SOUL, AND THOSE FEELINGS of confidence which accompany it, derive from those tranquil depths where God dwells and are proof of His presence there. They radiate from the Sun of Love within us, and are signs of His presence, though not its cause. That presence exists independently of the perceptible rays which betray it, and it is this that is our life.

God is clearly calling us to union with Him, and that union takes place in faith and not in sensible feelings. We must accustom ourselves by repeated acts to this life of faith, which places us very truly in contact with Him. But, needless to say, they are spiritual acts and it is a spiritual contact. We feel nothing, and we see and hear nothing. On the contrary, we are often completely plunged into a state of the most discouraging aridity. This is the soul's winter life. Nevertheless it is life, and a life we have to pass through. For this world is not Heaven, and exile is exile; and we must learn to accept it for as long as God wills, with all the attendant circumstances He wills. Such acceptance makes for union, and that is all that matters. Gradually, through these spiritual trials, we shall acquire our independence in regard to these circumstances, and by accepting them rise superior to them, and by grasping them grow stronger and so share in the strength of our divine Master, Jesus, Who has shown us the way.

Unhappily, people in general suffer from a great illusion in this regard. They imagine that detachment and strength consist in cutting themselves off from things; but this isn't true. True strength consists in avoiding absolutely what God wants us to avoid, and in accepting all that He wants us to accept—in other words, in abandonment to His divine Will. This is that holy indifference which is at the same time holy independence: the liberty of the children of God. The latter, to all appearance, live like everyone else, but interiorly they are very different. What dominates others, they dominate; and this because they want only God. Thus their will is not deflected, much less carried away: in other words, they are free.

The Holy Spirit, Who is the Spirit of the sons of adoption as He is of the only-begotten Son, will draw us more and more into this life of the spirit, and we will respond to that 'drawing' because we are souls of good will. *Peace to . . . men of good will.* That is why it is so important to base our lives on a spirituality which is deep. It is there, in those great depths where nothing can intrude, because they are the dwelling-place of Eternal Love, that we can always count on finding one another.

Believe Thus, and You Will Have Peace

∾∾

YES, YES: WE HAVE FOUND OUR REAL LIFE IN the depths of the soul, and we must hold on to it. This deeper life consists in an all-pervading peace, founded on faith in Divine Love. We believe that Infinite Love (and note well the word infinite— boundless—let it sink ever deeper) has seen us from all eternity, has loved us and wanted us; has given us being and life and maintains us therein; is directing our every step, overshadowing us at all times and in all places with the loving care of a father and mother; and is offering us increasingly all the ways that will unfailingly lead to union with Him. We believe that our weaknesses and spiritual miseries, our obstacles and difficulties, cannot prevent this union but, on the contrary, that God uses them as a means to bring about the realization of His love's designs.

This is the truth which should be the light of our life and our way to union. *Ego sum Via, Veritas et Vita . . . I am the Way, the Truth and the Life.* And so, one day, should He come and knock at the door of our soul already thus disposed, at once, by the very virtue of this habitual disposition, we shall answer: *I am ready*; and we shall set out upon our journey. Up to this moment, any kind of preoccupation is useless and only lessens our ardour. We must ruthlessly banish all doubts, then, from our life's path, replacing them immediately as soon as they appear by an act of faith in God's love. But do not confuse this act of faith with the feeling of faith: they are two distinct things. The former, which we must have, depends on us as well as on grace; the latter (the feeling) is the gift of God, independent of our will. When He bestows it, be glad and thank Him; when He does not, do not be distressed. In refusing it, He is still Love, and it is His love alone which is behind the refusal. Hold on to this faith and you will have peace, even if you do not feel it.

The Life of the Spirit, and our Everyday Existence

∽∾

IT IS ESSENTIAL, IN FACT, TO DISTINGUISH between these two lives, for they are utterly different. Yet they must not be kept apart; on the contrary, they should be brought together as much as possible. The life of the spirit should penetrate and impregnate and be the very life of our everyday existence. The secret, at once difficult and yet most consoling, is to know how to bring God into the very rhythm of our existence. Yet it is absolutely indispensable, but alas! all too rare. God is more present to us than we are to ourselves; or, if you think that too strong an expression, He is present to all that is deepest and most intimate in us. He is our real deep 'self'. He is one with it, and is unceasingly breathing life into that self, which would immediately fall back into nothingness, were it not constantly and in reality renewed. All our activity is born of this secret source, which is the Being of God within us.

Our life should consist quite simply in making and keeping contact with this divine Presence within us, which is God giving Himself. We ought to keep on saying to Him: 'My God, I believe in your presence in me; that you love me, and that you are giving yourself to me; and I want to respond to your love by giving you mine in return'. That is all we have to do. But this does not dispense us from living our ordinary external life (such as eating, sleeping and so on), which is brought into union with Him by a loving act of faith. Our everyday life can be what you will, but when it comes into contact with the soul it should be transformed—it should take on, that is, the soul's form. In a sickly body, or in any organ that is infected, the best of nourishment becomes harmful and even deadly. In a healthy soul, evil is changed into good, and what might cause death to the soul actually increases its life. And the reason is a very beautiful and encouraging one. We carry within us a principle of life, which is Life Itself giving life to everything. We see now the necessity for intimate union with God, and how essential it is for us every day to make continuous efforts to strengthen the ties that bind us more and more.

Strive your utmost, therefore, with this end in view, jealously to guard the peace of soul that God has been good enough to give you meanwhile. Don't worry about the way, nor as to what is happening; not even over much whether you will ever reach the end. Concern yourself solely with being with Him. We do not sufficiently reflect that before being our final reward, God is already our companion *in via*. He will be our reward, if we do our utmost to keep by His side. Then it is He Himself Who infuses our life and all its incidentals with His life, until we no longer live, but He lives in us.

Our Power

∽∾

OUR OWN GREAT ERROR AND THAT OF SO MANY
others these days is that we confuse feelings with
the soul. Feelings belong to the lower part of the
soul; they are the soul, but only in so far as it is
immersed in matter, and subject to all its fluctuat-
ing conditions. It is not the part that is truly and
properly speaking human. The human part is the
intellectual reason, which is superior to all the
lower part. The latter receives its light from above,
and should direct our whole being by means of
this purer light. Trials, fears, bitterness—these all
belong to the lower part; they have little to do with
our will. We cannot control them as we would like,
and we haven't that absolute authority over them
which needs only a word to restore peace and
drive away our troubles. We have only, so to say,
a political power, which communicates its loftier
views by a gradual influence.

In practice, our power is confined to two things,
and can only exercise itself in two ways:

(a) *By accepting.* 'My God, I accept and I offer
up to you this painful state, and my powerlessness
to alter it'. This we can always do, and it is an
enormous strength. Unfortunately we do not
appreciate what a power it is, and so we do not use

113

it, with the result that we lose priceless treasures. For see what happens. When we accept such and such a trial as from the hand of God and offer it up to Him, we are and we do what the priest does—we offer up a victim, and that victim is ourselves, and the offering is our very life itself. At that moment, our life and our being are offered up to God and lose themselves in Him, where we shall find them again *in aeternum*. What can we do that is greater or more beautiful than this? Thus we see the value and fecundity of our hours of anguish, and how many precious opportunities we lose daily.

(b) *The transformation which results from such acceptance.*

By virtue of accepting these trials as from the hand of God and offering them to Him, and by viewing them in this higher light, we come to see so much more easily their brighter side, and so find them much less painful. Trials take on for us a new aspect. But for this we must keep close to God, and that is why prayer and the sacraments are indispensable.

The Remedy for our Ills

∽∽

. . . THERE IS NO OTHER REMEDY FOR OUR PASS-
ing ills than God's eternal love for us. At bottom,
all our sufferings derive from the fact that we want
joy and possessions that are altogether too narrow
and fleeting for the greatness of our hearts.

Our Desire for the Infinite

ぬ

BE WITHOUT THE SLIGHTEST FEAR. OUR LORD Who has implanted in our hearts this desire for the infinite will never abandon us. He Himself desires infinitely to satisfy it. Our desire is but a mere spark from His, and it is His most vital gift to our souls. The more a soul suffers from it, the more of this gift has it received, and the greater it is. Our desires are our measure, and we are more or less what we desire. It is clear that these desires are a sort of seed, which Our Lord has cast into the soil of our souls, in order that it may develop. And the same love which has given the desire will also give the increase. It is sufficient that He find in us good will, for that is the good soil.

True Wisdom

HUMAN RELATIONSHIPS ARE AND ALWAYS WILL be a source of suffering. Even when we change our surroundings we do not change our soul with its responsiveness, nor the nature of our fellow beings, who are so often the cause of our sufferings. Life is too strong for us, and we must take it as a powerful force coming from God, and find Him in it. To kiss His hand, whether it caresses or wounds, is the only true wisdom.

Difficulties

❧

GUARD THE PEACE IN THE DEPTHS OF YOUR soul when you haven't it on the surface. The latter doesn't depend on us, but our deeper peace does. To desire peace is to possess it. The difficulties we have to contend with are not insurmountable; God proportions His grace according to our needs. We too often forget this, because we equally forget that God loves us. With all the force of His Infinite Being (which is the same as His Love) He wants us to belong to Him. He wants to give Himself to us, no matter the cost or the means, from always and for always. He places at the disposal of His love all the possibilities of His power and all the discernment of His wisdom. We can, therefore, trust Him in all our difficulties. Grace does not do away with the difficulties, but enables us to turn them to our profit. God has foreseen them all, and He has prepared aid for us which will make us stronger than them all. Why do we forget this aid, and look only at ourselves? No wonder we seem so weak and afraid. We have reason to be afraid of our weakness, but we are wrong to see that weakness without the help from God which is going to fortify us.

We must not be surprised at this fear, however. St Paul knew it, and asked God to remove the trial which was the cause of it. But God answered him: *My grace is sufficient for thee.* St Paul understood, and because He understood he added: *When I am weak, then am I powerful.* It is in my weakness that I find strength, but the strength of God that Jesus offers me is *that the power of Christ may dwell in me.*

Why Difficulties are Necessary

ᴄᴧᴄᴧ

WE MUST NOT BE SURPRISED AT THE DIFFICUL-
ties we encounter before we find peace. Difficulties
are necessary and precious. They are the exercises
by which our nature gets its training, and our
powers develop. A soul that did not meet with
them on its path would be greatly to be pitied. It
would remain for ever in its state of powerlessness.
We do not always realize that sufficiently. We want
to reach the goal without having run the course.
The 'running' is the effort, the exercise, the constant training, which brings into play our latent
powers and develops them through use. We must
find peace in these exercises, and love them as
God loves them; that is, as a means to an end, and
as remedies, at times bitter to the taste—even as
surgical operations!

Joy and Sadness

∽∽

WE MUST NOT BE SURPRISED AT FINDING THIS mixture of joy and sadness within us ... it is the same for everyone. Our nature is made up of two very different parts, and these two parts draw us in opposite directions, and seem to be in perpetual tension. It is our will which restores harmony by its acceptance of this state of things. Faith tells me: 'God wills this—*Deus vult*'. And my will, reacting immediately in union with His, answers: 'And I want it too: as He wants it and because He wants it'. This is the harmony we experience here below—a profound union of our being with God. And all superficial discords harmonize in this union with God Who permits them.

Viewed from this angle life is, as it were, a single line—indeed, less than a line. It is a simple movement, a single word. We live, and we constantly repeat the words: 'I will what God wills ... *Pater, fiat voluntas Tua*'.

This harmony between our will and God's does not prevent prayer. Indeed, prayer is part of it. I pray because God wants me to, and I accept in advance whatever answer He wishes to give to my prayer.

'Blessed are They that Mourn'

WE MUST NOT BE SURPRISED IF OUR PRAYER
has in it an element of sadness. It is no less prayer,
nor is it less powerful with God. God does not ask
us not to suffer; He asks us to 'take up our cross'
with both hands, and offer it up to Him in union
with His. Only later on shall we understand that
the times when He lays the cross on our shoulders
are the most precious moments of our lives.

*Blessed are they that mourn, for they shall be com-
forted.* Reflect often on the association of the words
'blessed' and 'they that mourn'. Clearly it is a
truth that is beyond us here below. In this life we
shall never see truth in all its fullness: we see it
only *in a dark manner*. That is why God has added
to the too feeble light of reason the light of faith,
which is a participation in His own light. He
increases this fuller light in us . . . and one day we
shall thank Him.

The Fiat *God Asks of Us*

❧

THE *FIAT* GOD ASKS OF US WHEN WE SUFFER IS not the *Fiat* of insensibility, but of suffering. When our heart is torn and continues to be so, we must give it to Him as it is. Later, when peace returns, we will give it to Him at peace. What He wants is for us to give ourselves to Him as we are. If there is anything to be put right He will do that, because we shall have handed ourselves over completely to Him.

On Worrying after Committing a Fault

～◌～

WORRYING AFTER COMMITTING A FAULT IS A
second fault, and adds to the first. It is even graver.
It was St Francis of Sales who used to say this,
and he knew what he was talking about. This is
the reason. A fault is an act against a virtue or a
commandment. Anxiety is contrary to the greatest
of all the commandments, as well as against the
queen of all the virtues. It is a sin against charity,
and against faith in the love of God. A person who
is anxious does not really believe in that love. For
belief in that love has the promise of eternal life.
*Qui credit in me habet vitam aeternam . . . he that
believeth in me hath everlasting life.* This is the very
centre of our life. Around it we should gather all
our mind's thoughts, all our heart's affections,
all our daily actions. As the saying is (and it is a
very true and beautiful one), we 'harmonize' them:
that is, we make harmony out of them.

That is, in fact, what the life of faith essentially
is—co-ordinated harmony. No matter how varied
its movements, and how replete with activity, it
remains always a unity. For it has God as its principle and term, and so partakes of His one-ness.
These various elements are only the material of
which life is composed, but that isn't life. Life is
the hidden principle which animates, co-ordinates,

124

directs and unifies all these elements. For the soul with real faith, this principle is the Holy Ghost.

Feelings in Ferment

ოო

OUR TROUBLES HAVE NOTHING TO DO WITH
our will. We do not seek them; we do not want
them, and we do nothing to bring them upon us.
In a word, they form no part in our moral (or
responsible) life. Our moral life consists in the
general trend of our thoughts and feelings, independent of those thoughts and feelings themselves.
We can let them into our moral life, but at the
peril of introducing fever and ferment. For that
is what they are—feelings in ferment. And this
accounts for our suffering. We are made for peace
and unity, and we would like everything to develop
into this harmonious unity. We would like our will
to impose its commands directly on the senses,
and the senses immediately to submit to the
mind's ascendancy. But that perfect submission no
longer exists since the Fall. We are at war with
ourselves. Re-read St Paul's Epistle to the
Romans, with its famous lament: *I see a law in my
members, fighting against the law of my mind . . . for
the good which I will, I do not; but the evil which I
will not, that I do . . . who will deliver me* (he
continues) from these evil tendencies? And he
answers composedly: '*The grace of God by Jesus
Christ*, Who came for that purpose—to restore the
order and unity that had been lost'.

126

But this isn't the work of a day: it's our life's task. We have to take up the struggle repeatedly and unceasingly; accepting the consequences of our divided nature (which can never find rest unaided), and pending its perfect restoration, declare war on them and put them to flight. Holy Scripture calls life a combat. We would be good soldiers of Christ . . . *bonus miles Christi*. It is in our hearts that the hardest battles will have to be fought, and it is against ourselves that we must obtain our victories. Fight, then, for Jesus, that His 'kingdom may come' in us. Don't ask where you are or what you are doing: forget yourself. A good soldier doesn't argue about the plan of a battle; he gets on with the battle! Our Lord's commands are our daily tasks, the state of our soul, the darkness and fears that make us afraid. Take yourself as you find yourself: give yourself as you are. Place all your trust in Him Who is directing the battle and is fighting in us, with us, and for us. *Nolite timere . . . Be not afraid; my peace I give unto you . . . I have overcome the world . . . Cast thy care upon the Lord . . . Come unto me all you that labour, and I will refresh you.*

Live 'In Conspectu Domini'

∾

EXTERNAL SERENITY—THAT IS TO SAY, THE necessary time—is needed for writing: interior serenity is not. So we must *make* it by acting in times of stress just as we would in a state of perfect tranquillity. This is where error and danger lurk for souls nowadays. It is obvious that we can write, and speak and act much better when our whole being is at peace. Activity, when we are tired and upset, is, it is quite certain, much more trying; it calls for much greater and often more painful effort. But strength of soul consists precisely in overcoming this difficulty and in making the effort, however painful; in acting, in a word, as if all were well. Nothing develops our moral character so much as effort of this kind, in which we pay no attention either to our sufferings, or to the pathetic poorness of the results. For even if the immediate results are poor, the long-term issue is worth while; for by forcing ourselves to act, despite the obstacles raised by our trying pre-dispositions, we acquire the habit of doing so almost always, and that saves an enormous amount of time. Always remember, then, that if we waited until we felt fit before acting, we would spend half our life-time waiting.

No, don't wait any longer for what, for some of

us, will never come. With the energy that each day brings, do the duty of the present moment, paying no heed to the result. That depends upon God; what depends upon us is the effort, and it is this effort which will gradually build up for us a strong will, and a co-ordinated and useful life.

Meanwhile pray very much, no matter what your dispositions or the circumstances. The trouble with all of us is that we fail to live in close, intimate and living contact with the source of the only true Life. Our sorrows come from that. Our helplessness discourages us, because we forget the all-powerfulness of God, Who is always ready to come to our aid. The evil in others as well as in ourselves, and the sad state of our times, all affect us only because we do not know how to keep ourselves in the presence of God, Who is infinite Goodness and overwhelming Joy. We do not know how to live *in conspectu Domini*.* Fortunately, God is drawing us and wants at all costs to possess Himself of us: it is His answer to our secret longing for Him. It is He Himself Who excites these secret longings and in due time satisfies them. It is in this sense that we can say that for souls of good will God does everything for them, so far as their spiritual life is concerned. Their will may be weak but it is good, really good (such a will always has been, and always will be good). We fail to think as

Translator's note: cf. Ps. cxviii: 168; *Because all my ways are in Thy sight.*

129

much as we should do how God's good Will (and that is His infinite love) has always overshadowed us, and always will. Don't expect to see the temptation or the weakness disappear, just because you have received the sacraments: the life of the soul is a slow growth. Keep in close touch with God, drawing on the resources of divine strength. A child eats and takes food, but does not turn into a man in a single day. Leave everything, therefore, to Him Who has the directing of your life, and is Himself your life.

Where We Must Seek Refuge

༄

WITH US, THE WORDS WE DO NOT SPEAK BE-
come prayers. There lies our strength, and we can
do no good except through this wonderful medium
of silence. We speak to God of those to whom our
lips are closed. We must ask God for the grace
to find ourselves, instead of running away from
ourselves. To find ourselves, or to run away from
ourselves—these are mere figures of speech. What
they signify, and the truth deeper than themselves
in which they find their true interpretation, is this.
There is within us the object of our aspirations.
He is truly there, in a manner personal and living:
like a brother, a friend and a father; giving Himself
intimately and continuously. He is our true being;
that part of ourselves which is not carried away at
every moment by the current of life; that part that
is unchanging and eternal. To find oneself is to
find God in oneself. This discovery is the work of a
loving faith. Souls that love have a way of believing
which, as it were, takes them out of themselves
and draws them into the object of their faith. The
word of the Gospel is easy to them: *If anyone love
me, he will keep my word, and we will come to him
and will make our abode with him.* That is where
we must seek refuge, and where we shall find ourselves—in the soul's centre where God abides. And

when we have found God within us and have made Him the beloved companion of our days and hours, life will no longer be so burdensome to us or the society of our fellow creatures so irksome. We shall see and love, in them as in ourselves, Him Who is the Source of all beauty.

This interior life will likewise enable us to do good to others round about us. That is what is lacking in those who haven't the Faith. They are unable to love Him and to unite themselves with Him, Who alone can fill the void in their hearts, and give them the perfection of which we dream. Perfection is the intimate handiwork of Love giving Himself; our daily perfection is what that Love does each day. It is only relative and imperfect, but the effort, repeated again and again, will one day render it absolute and perfect.

The Cleft in the Rock

∽∽

WHY THESE ALTERNATING PERIODS OF PEACE
and storm? Why this succession of joys and sorrows? There is only one answer, and it is the definition itself of God: *Deus caritas est . . . God is Love.*
All that God does or permits is from a motive of
love. We must get this idea firmly rooted in our
minds; or, better still, establish ourselves in it, as
in a kind of fortress. The reason we are so violently
shaken by interior storms or annoyances from outside is because we have not yet found this *Cleft in
the Rock*. Outside this shelter, what is there except
our own poor wretchedness? It is obvious that
we cannot put up any resistance. That is where we
shall find the remedy of our too sensitive reactions.
We have attempted it, and that is already a first
grace. But we mustn't leave it at that: it must be
repeated so frequently that it becomes a habit,
and, as it were, the normal trend of our spiritual
life. No matter what the circumstances, we must
turn to Him Who is Truth and Life. If we are
happy, we are happy in Him; if we suffer, then we
turn to Him, so that He may at the same time
help us to bear our suffering and sanctify it.

Silence

∾

SILENCE AND MEMORY GO WELL IN HAND. WE
know that silence is not a void, but on the contrary
by its very nature a fullness; but a plenitude in
which our thoughts are made known. Speech that
is the result of bustle and noise is bound to be
superficial. The seat of silence should be the
depths of our being, and that 'being' only utters
something true and profound when it comes from
that silence, and is its expression.

That is why the world's speech—conversations,
the press and so on—is so fatuous and wearying,
instead of being restful and beneficial. That is why,
on the other hand, in Charterhouse one experi-
ences such peace. There, everything emanates
from the calm depths of the soul, where all is
recollected and silent. That is where God abides
and where we infallibly find Him, if we abide there
too. Not everyone, obviously, because of the circumstances of their lives, can experience that same
recollection that exists in a Charterhouse, but they
must not be afraid to set aside as far as possible
at least some moments, however short, for recollection, and to give some time to Him Who is
within them. It is in that silence that He speaks to
us, and bids us listen to Him.

In Charterhouse

∽∾

In Charterhouse—that is, for a Carthusian—a change of house or monastery does not surprise us or disturb us. Our life is the same pilgrimage to Heaven, continued under other skies. The goal remains the same, and the same Light is guiding us.

Peace is the great blessing—the blessing of blessings; the blessing of God that we are constantly praying for: our *requiem aeternam*. It makes us see all things in the light of the God of peace. It shows us that ultimately *everything* is subject to His laws; that even those movements which tend to draw us away from Him are made to enter into His plan of glory and contribute to its realization. Once we have understood that, then nothing disturbs us, nor ever can disturb us any more . . .

Biblical References in the Text

❧